Other Titles by the Author

Fiction

Cows, Gods and Cannon Fodder

Avenging Angels and Earthly Gods

The Authors Itch

Other

Poems, Prose and Pictures
A Practical Guide to Practically Nothing

This book is dedicated to anyone who still retains the ability to engage in a simple quiet moments without multitasking on a phone.
Trust me; there aren't many of us left

Free Advice for a Price

or

Zen Moments of an Absurd Mind

By

Lionel Strong

There are many reasons to write.
Perhaps a history needs be told, or a life story related.
Perhaps there is need to impart knowledge of some obscure topic to an audience, willing or not, or simply instruct a prospective pupil in a new way of doing something.
Some even find the need to put pen to paper to relive personal experiences or, construct from within their fertile minds, a work of fiction.
It matters not the reason, everyone, at some time in their existence feels a need to put pen to paper or as is now so often the case keyboard to social media.
Truth is we all want to be heard.
Why else would someone choose to bore the pants of their six hundred 'friends' with every aspect of their daily existence or spend years toiling in the basement compiling a tome on how they won the war.
We want to be heard, no, we need to be heard!
After all we are human and humans communicate!
OK, that's rubbish, but it sounds good.
The fact is, we humans only talk to each other when we want something.
Groceries, ground, love, affection, property, order, sympathy and disciples are just some of the reasons we feel the need to actually talk with our fellow human beings and if those brief moments of communication don't solve our needs or problems we generally resort to aggressive behaviour, all-out war or sulking.
If it were at all possible to exist totally within our minds without need for any form of exterior contact we would do so.

We are internal creatures who simply react to the input of the world around us.
We have friends because it is much safer than having enemies.
We have lovers because we are chemically driven to do so, it makes us feel good and having someone else permanently at your side provides security, wards of insecurity and doubles the income.
We relate with employers, shopkeepers, friends and everyone else because they all supply us with what we need to keep the electrical processor in our skulls purring, and the mechanical body that carts it around working to keep the system in operational order.
Religion falls into the area of a failsafe mechanism, there to promise a continuation of the operating system when the mechanics fail.
We are solo brains bent on achieving nourishment, nurturing, protection and stimulation and if we need a mass audience of other solo brains around us to get the job done then so be it.
Now if this all sounds a little too clinical then I am sorry but the reality is, that is how the world works.
Every need, every emotion, every aspect of our supposedly in control lives is nothing more than a survival reaction to our environment. The best we can actually do is go along for the ride, pray, and try to find logical ways to inhabit the mechanical
world without going either nuts or accidently killing ourselves.
And therein rests the reason for this book.
My Zen moment.

Life's little lessons, quirks and enlightenments as perceived by self, pared down to four lines or less, because too many words tend to cloud the meaning, put to paper, then hurled out there into the cosmos.
The world we live in, the life we live, how to survive it, what we are all about, the unanswered questions and all the other crap according to me, my brain and I, all there for you to read and ponder if for no other reason than to light a candle of curiosity that leads to a little more thinking.
After all, if we all spent more time thinking and less time talking, the world would be a much quieter, safer place and that can't be all bad.
So please, sit back, take in each of my small offerings, ponder them, dissect them, decide if I am correct, incorrect, stupid, irrelevant, brilliant or just a nutter with too much time on his hands and then move onto the next. The worst that can happen is that you spend a few hours concentrating on the absurdness of my life thereby removing yourself for a brief moment from the absurdity of your own.

May you live long and ponder

L. Strong

'Hits Sageems Si Newtirt Ni Doce'

And so we begin:

1. We exist in self. Free roaming the multiverse of our minds. Only held back by external distractions and required systems maintenance.

2. Within my brain, lies a brain, safe behind a window pane. A brain that no one else can see, the inner brain that makes a me, me.

3. Stress is the result of the immovable object meeting the unrelenting annoyance.

4. Happiness is achieved by ignoring the bleeding obvious reality in favour of the irrationally impractical fantasy.

5. Tomorrow, when the world has moved a little further to the left, people will still feel the need to be right.

6. There are many intersecting roads. Some go right, some go straight ahead, and some go wrong. Learn to pause and read the signs.

7. I am Shakespeare without the turn of phrase, gift of prose, knowledge of the world or theatrical talent. 'Alas poor William, I do thee not well'

8. At any second the ground could crack open and swallow you up, the air could crow cold and freeze your innards, or the sun could explode and toast your flesh. And you thought you were in control!

9. Begin by asking the question, take time to think about the answer then proceed with cautious enthusiasm. If you can't, then either ask another question or move in another direction..

10. If anyone tells you that there is no such thing as infinity simply ask them to look into the night sky and point out to you the edges.

11. Everything we know is only relevant to us.

12. Let us hope we are never visited by superior beings because if we were they would surely declare us vermin and commence the cull.

13. If god made us in his own image then he must surely be an overweight, skinny, good looking, ugly bi sexual with a cruel but compassionate disposition.

14. Once we rode on the turtles back and the world was flat. Now we ride on an internet and declare our knowledge supreme. What fools are we who refuse to see that we cannot see everything.

15. The funniest joke is recognizing the futility of existence for the first time. If one can't laugh at our own fragility what can one laugh at?

16. Sitting on the seaside sweating up the sun as seagulls swoop over sandy shores. Everything to excess.

17. There is nothing worse than waiting in line with people who do not want to wait in line.

18. I am sorry if I insult you. I was simply trying to offend you.

19. If the universe if infinitely large cannot it also be infinitely small and if so where on the scale do we sit.

20. Words said cannot be repealed. Words never said cannot be questioned. Is it better to say what you think or think what you would like to say?

21. Lord, grant me the patience to wait until you answer and the good sense to question when you do.

22. I only know which way is up because I can perceive a down

23. If you read it on the internet then it may well be very nearly true.

24. Faith is reading the side effects leaflet on a drug and taking it anyway.

25. Waiting in line is the prerogative of the poor.

26. I have a dog! Sorry, I mean my dog has a human.
I have a cat! Sorry, I mean my cat has a pet.
If you own a dog then buy a cat. That way you can have a method of comparing love with indifference.

27. Only throw away those things that are not alive. With the exception of cats.

28. Never tread in other peoples puddles

29. When you wake each day check if you are dead.
 If you aren't then get off your lazy arse and live.
 If you are then feel free to sleep in

30. Computers are just us staring at us.

31. Children are the receptacles of our failings.
        Feed them well

32. Sometimes looking at others is less important than   looking at ourselves.

33. Never open your mouth until you have something to say and have rehearsed how to say it.

34. I only know what I know because someone before me said it.

35. The river curses rocks and sails on in confusion. The rocks sleep in silence. Be a rock.

36. My left foot rests.
    My right advances then rests
    My left advances and rests.
     Mutually beneficial cooperation.

37. Temper comes as clouds of grey that bar
    the way till blown away.

38. An autumn leaf falls, then all, then none.
        Then back to where it all began
          Such is everything.

39. A mother listens and smiles. A Father
    smiles and listens. Same but different.

40. On my plate rest red and green with
    something dead in between. Is that
    obscene?

41. We come in peace their leader said. With knowledge held in books. We sent them home in pieces. We didn't like their looks.

42. Budda sits upon my bench, a wise and worthy master. He chooses not to talk to me because he's made of plaster.

43. My coffee it is cold now, I made it sit and wait, I should have drunk it sooner, but now it is too late.

44. No matter how fast the gazelle may go the same sun will shine on the tortoise slow.

45. A flickering candle can only be seen in a breeze but its light can be seen in the still of night

46. Until I finally open the can, it could be peas it could be spam.

47. Finding treasure in my yard, wasn't really very hard, all I had to do was sit and listen to the deafening silence of everything.

48. The sun will rise tomorrow. Have faith and patience. If it doesn't, have a shovel.

49. He drinks to forget until he forgets to drink.

50. I wear a hat, it covers my hair. I wear my hair it covers my head. I wear my head it covers my inadequacies.

51. A blackbird flying by at night may be there or may not.

52. News comes news goes. When it ends only news knows

53. I peeled an orange. Sour and bitter. Anticipation overtaken by reality.

54. My paper has lines. Even when I write I am expected to conform.

55. If it needs to be cleaned use a washing machine. Any friend will do.

56. The heater blows on my head. Brain boils in silence. Toes demand equality.

57. Bananas come in family groups. Appealing!

58. Sit with your back to me please. I need to be ignored by you

59. A hat sits on my coffee table. Somewhere a head feels undressed.

60. No rain today, just clouds. I await their tears.

61. My candle is unlit as is my match. Sad that one must suicide so the other may shine.

62. Children argue and I withdraw. Children argue and I withdraw more. Children argue and I withdraw no more. Such is war.

63. My blinds are nearly open. Morning creeps in.
    > I close them.
    > Too late!

64. What use is a chair without a passenger?

65. Catalogues come, catalogues go, what I actually need,
    nobody knows.

66. Roses bloom in summertime, sticks in winter, undecided in between.

67. Is my son loud or am I intolerant. I ponder. Or at least I would were it not for the damn noise.

68. Dust on my pillow. Yesterday's dreams or dandruff?

69. I am not cynical but I will be soon.

70. My tea is cold, as is the night, so under blanket I creep, yet I do not sleep.

71. Only corn grows in my garden. Perhaps I should use different seeds.

72. My dog barks at birds, my dog barks at cats, my dog barks at strangers, and sleeps
    My cat, having no need for a bark, sleeps

73. I took a little pill today, to make my headache go away. Perhaps I should have done instead, was remove the rubbish from my head.

74. I have two phones. They both get messages. Double the opportunity to have unwanted conversations with friends I don't know..

75. The internet enables everyone to know everything without need for verification.

76. Where is the logic when we keep drugs that might kill you in a chemist and cigarettes that will kill you in a supermarket?

77. Quiet streets of lonely people. Pavements footless. A siren wakes the sleeping. Lights come on. Someone hides in the shadows. A body. A novel!

78. The elm leans lazily, a west wind its foe. Bow and sleep lest you stand and weep.

79. My eyes see independently. My brain cannot compensate. New glasses needed.

80. The old man looked down. Currency on the ground. Elation at recovery. Unease at possible discovery.

81. No two stones are the same. Pray prove me wrong.

82. I can sleep while others weep yet still I dream of tears.

83. Bottom line is this may be our last chance, for sure!

84. I love small things in a really big way.

85. My son thinks the world was built just for him. Maybe he is Jesus?

86. A long time ago is a different long time ago to an adult and a child.

87. Never forget that remembering is part recollection, part reconstruction and part stab in the dark.

88. Only on sunny days can you look out and wish it was raining.

89. If I am down it is only because my spade was too large and my digging skills to good.

90. I know me not nearly as well as I know who I would like to be.

91. Decimals were invented to mock people with nine fingers.

92. Come in, sit down, we are all equals here. Sorry that's my chair!

93. Dictionary spelt backwards is yranoitcid and means reading words in reverse, which is now, because it is in a book, a word and as such deserves an entry.

94. The river rises with the rain then falls again. The river rises with the rain. Until it doesn't. Precedents!

95. She washes, then sorts, then stacks, then irons. They dirty, crease and toss. She washes. No slaves here. Just mothers and children.

96. Make time to laugh, make time to play, make time to think, make time to be you. If you can't then buy a better watch.

97. Clouds drift past in grey suits. No rain today, just shadows and the occasional golden finger.

98. I laugh, she laughs. I smile, she smiles. Nothing much wrong here.

99. My car goes where I point it which is more than you can say for my brain.

100. A rose arose and roared. Not to be ignored a posy posed and postulated. War of the poser roses.

101. Never let children tell you they don't know, after all for most of the time they insist they know everything

102. A bean is but an unfulfilled destiny.

103. My mind wants to yell. My self wants to hide. Whom do I protect whom do I reject?

104. At sixteen she was pregnant, at seventeen she was mom, at eighteen she was abandoned, at nineteen she was gone. A life in three lines.

105. A million, million leaves sway gently on a breeze as a billion, billion insects do exactly as they please.

106. A moron is an idiot with half the brain of a cretin and the potential of a god.

107. A fence runs over the valley, it ambles north to south, there to keep the sheep inside and nosey humans out.

108. Never throw a rock if you cannot catch.

109. Dogs bark at shadows to keep the beast at bay. People yell at everything and then they go and pray.

110. Children, contrary to popular opinion are not cute. Children however can be cute providing the price is right.

111. I only want things I do not have, which defeats the purpose of having everything.

112.   Never let it be said I did not ask the hard questions nor found many answers too hard to accept.

113.   Sport is the thing you do when you wish to demonstrate that you are the best at something that achieves nothing.

114.   The outlook does not bode well for the human race when you consider that historically things have gone pretty bad for people who shot second and asked questions first.

115.   My toes like dark warm places and my socks are claustrophobic which is why I wear them with thongs.

116. Light is faster than everything except the stuff we can't see. Science fact!

117. He who thinks there is honour in war should be the first made to pick up a gun.
He who finds no honour in war should wave the flag as the   honourable leave.

118. I once one. I won once. Both at the same time.

119. Music is conversation for the ears only

120. Be happy that you are able to record what is written then go write something to make others happy

121. Shed a tear for the man who owns only one shoe but does not limp

122. Old people are just young people who know younger people

123. It's nice to be in charge. Trouble is most of the time we just think we are.

124. A CEO is simply someone with enough clout to survive the fallout from their decisions.

125. Money can't buy happiness. It can however buy pretty much everything else.

126. I love small miracles and unexpected outcomes. Rarities in a world of norms.

127. Have you ever picked up a leaf and wonder why it chose to leave home?

128. A queue is a line of expectation wrapped in a blanket of impatience.

129. Sixty cents. Just close enough to a dollar to remain relevant but inadequate.

130. If I hide inside will I still be able to see out?

131.   I have lost the ability to comprehend what I have lost.

132.   Truth is a story told in such a way that it cannot be disputed.

133.   I want half! The other two thirds you can split between the four of you.

134.   Waiting in a hospital is like standing on a freeway blindfolded. You know eventually you are going to get attention, but the outcome could be fatal.

135.   There is sickness and illness. Illness requires an ailment. Sickness only requires a distracted mind.

136. Only stand on mountain tops if you have no fear of falling.

137. I eat and eat which means my mind is far hungrier than my body.

138. Only a self-centred person can be given a rose and turn it into a briar.

139. Lest old acquaintances be something or other?

140. Only sit after the chair has been vacated.
To do otherwise may be see you arrested

141. Santa comes but once a year. If he came more often we would be broke I fear.

142. My watch contributes nothing which begs the question why do we all slavishly follow time.

143. Why is it I lose the ability to remember things I wish not to forget and retain the ability to remember things best forgotten?

144. Please do not speak to me until after I have considered my response to your lack of response.

145. A hammer is of little use to someone without a nail unless their intent is to tear down your house.

146. The soles of ones feet newer know rain much the same as the top of the head never knows puddles.
Each to their own!

147. If I stand here and queue will you take me with you?

148. I enter a room of decorations all wearing ties.

149. Above me the wind blows. I think of willows.

150. I wear gloves to protect my hands from not wearing gloves.

151. A fire is lit in the hills. It has been a wet year

152. I reject your argument but accept your conclusion.

153. Red is the colour you paint a blue sky in the evening.

154. If here is where I am then where am I when I am not here?

155. A blade of grass cuts only air

156. If the tap is off and the water still flows then review ones thinking.

157. I wash my hands and my day vanishes.

158. Little do we know how little we do know

159. Supercala, blah, blah, blah, blah, blah, blah, ocious.
The melody lingers on while the memory is long gone.

160. Mice mainly eat cheese. Sadly not! Another childhood vision dashed.

161. Light a match to light a candle to show the way to another match.

162. For a seed to grow it must firstly escape that which surrounds it.

163. I have two sons. One ten going on thirty. One eight going on four. I am sixty five going on worn out.

164. My blinds are closed and yet my windows are open.

165. I awake every morning until I do not.

166. The job is easy! It's life that's hard. Little training, no manual.

167. If my dog barks at night I cry out for silence and yet I keep a watch dog. Confusion for my canine.

168. My tea is too hot so I wait. To soon brings pain, too long leads to disappointment. Strange, that we can't discover 'just right' without experiencing both.

169. Sun soaks my morning. I write. Two clocks break my silence. A mechanical conversation now lost to many.

170. It rains, it stops, it rains. I go in, go out, and go in.
 Oh to be part amphibian!

171. Up in the sky a bird flies by. Down on the ground we stumble around, look up and sigh.

172. She sits and plays. Fingers caress screen. I dread the onslaught of flat battery.

173. The needle shows the way, the thread sows the way.

174. Fire blazes warm, family and cats sleep close, wood brings harmony.

175. It is Monday. A beginning. Time to put aside the past and push on to Saturday and a pause in the road

176. Forecasters say rain, rain, rain. I open my blinds and see sun, sun, sun, sun.
Still I live with the expectation of accuracy.

177. My floor looks like tiles. It is not. Which begs the question 'if you like the look why not use the real thing'

178. Bread enters toaster, get burnt, and becomes toast. Food goes into the oven, gets burnt, and becomes rubbish. We truly are a strange species

179. Our cricket team won a great victory! Poverty remains, wars still rage, and life for many is still a struggle. Perhaps the victory was not so great?

180. My dog roams free in the park. Canine happiness versus the catcher.

181. My car boot is full with Christmas. My pockets are empty from Christmas. Stupidity trumps common sense

182. My wife calls our dog. He doesn't understand English until his work is done or the word biscuit is used.

183. There are bullies in our street; I do not want to meet, until I get much older which is when they will be beat.

184. I shall now meditate on nothing. Didn't work!

185. Where do you go when the one you wish to escape from is yourself?

186. If all life is precious why do we hoard gold and undervalue compassion?

187. If I am not meant to write why do the words invade my brain and my fingers recognize the keys?

188. My son smiles and asks for treats. I smile and decline. War is declared. A treaty is reached. I get peace, he gets treats.

189. Immortality lies within the pages of a written work providing there is no need for something to burn.

190. I have a knife for everything but I usually only use two which begs the question in which areas am I not cutting it

191. Santa came to our street in a fire truck. Hose, hose, hose!

192. I do not believe in Santa, his reindeer or his loot. Which leads me now to ponder who is the bastard in the suit?

193. The Mayan calendar ended and we are all still here which means the purveyors of doomsday should have chosen a better year.

194. Christmas is coming the rich are getting fat. The middle class are struggling while the poor pass round the hat.

195. If green is the shade of tomorrow tinted with patches of blue why do we spray paint with rubbish and think that colour it will do.

196. If you are old. More departed than arriving. Pray for a slower train.

197. I think Zen, which is not Zen as Zen is not thinking therefore, I am not Zen.

198. Dogs like bones. I like dogs. Dogs like me. I don't like bones. One of us won't starve.

199. Just because I know the difference between right and wrong doesn't mean I accept the concept.

200. Smarmy seagulls rarely sail swiftly over stormy seas.

201. A nail hammered without care often needs to restart its journey.

202. I cannot hold to the concept of a single creator without raising the concept of a creator's creator.

203. Little did I know that the little I did know was too little!

204. Warm inside, cold out. Cold inside, warm out. Hard to define a person who wishes to remain hidden.

205. Must warm feet on a cold day. I rush to fire. An outcome defeated by lack of matches

206. Watch for walls that bar your way. Carry your own doors. Help others find an opening.

207. Saw a doctor today. She was feeling ill. Irony?

208. Watch for the plans of others. They tend to revise without notice.

209. It is hot! Damn hot! I complain but still haven't the sense to go inside.

210. Only the sun could look down on humanity and get a warm feeling.

211. A day of fires, wild winds and waiting. Some fight, some flee, some hide with nowhere to go and the clouds of salvation remain absent.

212. We all shit, we all piss. The poor, the rich, the educated, the ignorant and the gods. I fear there are no individuals here.

213. Alas poor Yorick, I know not your story.

214. Why, when god said "let there be light" did we still choose to remain in the dark.

215. My legs chose to move before my ears told them the direction they should be going and I paid the price of favouritism.

216. I am as you see me and yet this is only the me that I choose for you to see.

217. As I write between the lines I ponder on who invented the lines I write between?

218. No one wants to be the first to be last

219. I fear that many of the things I see may only exist within my imagination and my mind has no way of telling the difference.

220. The older I get the less I fear being seen as being stupid. A reversion to my childhood.

221. I cannot see beyond my own horizon.

222. Truth is always told with a touch of embellishment.

223. We always look to others to confirm our reference.
    Choose your friends wisely.

224. There is black and white! Your black and white, my black and white and a possible middle ground.

225. A coin tossed has at least four outcomes. Heads, tails, neither, lost. We should always seek out alternative options.

226. In my mind lies all the knowledge of the universe providing it remains in my mind.

227. I am at war with an eight year old. He is amused by my frustration. He is well defended, I am under resourced. Such is the futility of parenting.

228.　Yesterday hot, today cold. Enough of me lets discuss the weather.

229.　My mind is questioned by another. The predicament is how to define if it is them or me doing the questioning. Reality is a bitch!

230.　If I talk of me I am in the moment. If others talk of me I live forever. There is good and bad in there.

231.　She spends a year planning a birthday. A glorious entry to 21. A total waste of 20.

232.　The winds blow to the west. All dragons chase their tails.

233. I live in a small box, in a box of boxes in a carton of boxes in a container of cartons in an empty room.

234. All prophets were born of women and yet no women are prophets. Why? Could it be because men invented prophets?

235. There is nothing about sex that cannot be explained by watching two dogs but try doing the same thing with love.

236. Up in the air a leaf drifts by, a tree droops and cries, the seasons change as children leave.

237. Most people are too busy seeking a destination to see the signs along the way.

238. From a head of wheat comes a green field or a loaf of bread. Eat wisely!

239. Walk with your head held high and watch for low branches

240. Only a fool puts both feet in the same puddle

241. If I left you standing there, would you worry, would you care, and if I returned after a while, would you frown or would you smile

242. The day is cool. Ashes lie sleeping. No smoke today. We await a warm hug.

243. Many cars pass in convoy. Some peel off, some slide in, others sit awaiting directions.

244. I awoke to sunshine. Found a cloud. Wrapped it around me as a shroud. Waited for the rain to come, but instead found the sun.

245. Life is like dreaming except the pain is more intense

246. Sometimes I live in a dream and wake up in a nightmare

247.   Bushfires burn everything. Aggressive non-discrimination.

248.   An aboriginal is someone who was here before we were here, but was here after those that were here before they were here.

249.   He who smiles in the face of adversary is either stupid or has no concept of his predicament.

250.   I see little benefit in telling a wise man he is wrong.

251.   Snails move as slowly as you would if you had no limbs

252. If you tell me what I did right I will like you. If you show me what I did wrong I will respect you.

253. There is no peace to be found in combat.

254. All hail the king for he has the power to rain on your parade.

255. My son is bored. A condition I have called annoying.
    My son has ADT. A condition I have called Absolutely Debilitating Temperament.

256. Blinds open the world sees in. blinds closed I see in.

257. I have twenty keys, six locks. Inventory saved without purpose.

258.   She holds all her history in her purse. Memories kept close to define self.

259.   I sit and wait so that I may move on to sit and wait.

260.   If ever I say I give up, please do not give up, as I am only telling you what I would do.

261.   I have never been so sure that I am unsure.

262.   Today my feet walked a hundred miles, my body five and my mind is still out there slogging away.

263. Oh to be a six year old dreaming I was sixty.

264. Why do angels have wings?

265. I awake. It is six am. Over prepared, underwhelmed, I leave.

266. Doctors paint her pink and prod. They photograph and nod. Diagnosis made they talk a secret language to a child.

267. I sit in a ray that uses my window as a door

268. A spider walks along its ground. Looks up and sees me upside down.

269. I wear runners everywhere and yet I do not run.

270. I awake to a television telling me everything I would prefer not to know.

271. Outside my window is a freeway used by those who are neither free or know their way.

272. I drink water from a bottle. Same water different tap.

273.   We deny what might happen so that we might appear surprised when it does.

274.   Experience has taught me that I sink far better than I swim.

275.   I used to think I was short until one day I realized everyone else was tall.

276.   If I know I am dead then there is a god.

277.   Consider the possibility that I am part of your dream.

278. I believe that I am as sane as any other Martian

279. I put butter on bread so my tomato won't make it go soggy then; I put it in my mouth and chew until it is soggy enough to swallow. Go figure?

280. I am constantly thinking about everything which tends to confuse my focus

281. We think we are eagles when in fact we are all Dodos.

282. The way out is usually the same as the way in.

283. As we get older we do less of most things except deny that we can do less

284. We fail to comprehend that we are made of the very same stuff we try so hard to wash away.

285. The only thing that can stop a river is a lack of water.

286. I fear that if I could ever comprehend how I think I would end up

doing nothing else except thinking about thinking.

287. A mountain is never as imposing if viewed from a higher mountain.

288. The circle of life is more a wavy crinkly line with lots of angles, wrong turns and dead ends.

289. I fart because I no longer need that which wishes to leave.

290. My clock stopped. My life goes on.

291.   Today the sun rose. As long as I rise tomorrow it will do it again.

292.   Fifty percent off the second item denotes a society stuck on wants over needs.

293.   Would a blind man be better off if the traffic drove on the footpath and he walked on the road?

294.   Running out of air would have less a long term effect on us than would running out of electricity.

295.   Anyone who can live without the attention of others is dead.

296. Why is it that the cake in the window always tastes better than the cake in the mouth?

297. Only a wealthy man builds a house then buys a hammer.

298. A duck would make a lousy cow!

299. Bacteria are superior while we remain inferior

300. A small ant walks past. I notice him he doesn't notice me. My size makes me insignificant.

301. I would listen to the world if I only understood the language

302. Mankind has never built anything worthy of being left behind for another species except piles of shit for seagulls.

303. Mobile phones promise freedom but deliver prison.

304. Better to walk barefoot than to try fill another's shoes.

305. God arrived in messenger form. Needed a briefing. So much for all seeing.

306. My wings no longer support me. I am doomed to walk amid the chickens.

307. The only difference between king and pauper is that the king has someone to flush for him.

308. Never open a door that cannot be closed makes far more sense than never close a door that can't be opened.

309.   I have many more questions than answers and yet I am continually expected to know the answer to everything.

310.   Most individuals think alike.

311.   Lest we forget that which we should have remembered.

312.   Only one way is the wrong way once you have chosen it.

313.   A blade of grass is as important in the scheme of things as a forest.

314. Everything you know is subject to the knowledge of others unless you just make shit up

315. And man created gods in his own image.

316. Confusion is the result of a lack of knowledge combined with a lack of comprehension

317. The art of warfare is something we perfect as a child and stuff up as an adult.

318. The chicken came first because the egg couldn't

319. The saddest thing I have learnt is that someone else has already thought all my thoughts.

320. A computer will not save you when the lights go out.

321. The more affluent we become the less we are able to protect ourselves.

322. Religion is one part faith, one part text and three parts someone else's interpretation.

323. A good hymn is a song sang to relieve the boredom from words said. A bad hymn is the dead space between the lord said and   amen.

324. Never let it be said that I did not let you say it.

325. Birds have wings to escape the ground hugger

326. Even people who plan ahead have need for a leap of faith.

327. I am both ill and sick

328. I see no reason to argue with anyone who tells me I am wrong

329. Why is it that a smile or the word please are so different but generally elicit much the same response?

330. Duck!
Quack, quack, quack, wack!
Didn't!

331. I seek to find reason in everything but generally only find my mind.

332. My rational side says I am in control. My irrational side agrees.

333. Tribal warfare in a modern world involves children playing, parents cheering them on.

334.   How can you win when losing is the goal?

335.   If I wanted to know what you thought I would have thought to ask you.

336.   Alas, damn! has been usurped by fuck!

337.   My delusional self tries to influence the thoughts of others by thinking. Problem is their reception confuses my transmission.

338.   I like sex almost as much as I like thinking about sex...............and chocolate

339. I listen to you because I hate solitude, then I don't.

340. Holding ones breath long enough teaches one how to lie down.

341. Don't be stupid! Just be you.

342. The sad thing is that if I sold my children I would just have to go out and buy more.

343.   I look up and see sky. I look down and see ground. I conclude that I am just fill!

344.   If you wish to know your significance in the scheme of things just sit down and write a list of how many of the six billion other inhabitants of this rock you know personally.

345.   I do not understand why you do not understand and frankly I have neither the time nor energy to find out.
Now that's how you start a war!

346.   Words not said stay in the head.

347. I may mean what I say but that in no way means that I say what I mean.

348. Sometimes I realize that the mountain I stand on is a very deep dark place.

349. Am I? Am I the same person as I was yesterday? I am I think, or am I? Now I am really confused.

350. It's just a brief walk from womb to tomb.

351. Travelling lone wolves rarely pack.

352. Today I came to the realization that someone was in charge and it wasn't me.

353. Is it a comforting thought that kings, Queens and captains of industry all end up as eroded indecipherable scratches on a marble blocks

354. Never be afraid to say what you think but always be prepared to accept the consequences.

355. At the end of each driveway is a road to somewhere.

356. Patience is a virtue, frustration is the cost

357. If I am old then I am still here.

358. If you wish to leave something behind then let it be a clean room.

359. I was never invited, so why should I go?

360. My dog understands me yet he knows no English.

361. A blog is just and ego with somewhere to go.

362. An epitaph: Hold over my bones for a later date lest someone should find them a better fate

363.   I hold out for a miracle whilst pondering a solution.
    I hold out for a solution whilst pondering an excuse.
    I offer an excuse whilst planning an exit.
    I give up on an exit and hold out for a miracle.

364.   Today the sun shone! The weather was miserable, the sky dark and wet, but the sun shone.

365.   Mud is nothing without clean water.

366.   I am told I am old by others who are on my road heading south.

367.   I have entered the lazy period that falls between idleness and apathy.

368.   I have discovered that my mind is nothing without a quest.

369.   Not a day goes by without a day going by.

370.   I am involved with me and I like it.

371. I never thought I would have so many thoughts

372. Every time I write down what I think, I end up thinking about why I thought what I thought.

373. There is moss over there! Rocks are lazy bastards.

374. I have found that in my attempts to display my youthfulness I am continually usurped by my body.

375. I am confused! Proof again that I am human.

376. A wonderful weekend was had by all. Pity about the rest of us.

377. I await a sign. Any sign. Even if I don't know what it means.

378. My cat sleeps for eighteen hours, meditates for three, and eats than harasses my dog. Oh to be a cat.

379. Lofty ideals lead to bumpy landings for dreamers.

380. Sometimes surrender is the best form of attack.

381. Everyone looks so sad. Must be a day ending in Y.

382. Sometimes I wonder what it is all about. Then I don't.

383. There are perspectives and then there is my view. I accept the former and adapt it to suit the latter.

384. Just once I would like to be told by someone that I am correct.

385. Never let logic get in the way of supposition in case truth breaks out

386. A flame burns just a brightly in the mind of a blind man.

387. Recycling: the way we put back what we never should have taken.

388. A just war is one that is over before a shot is fired.

389. Only small ideas can infect an ignorant mind.

390.   An ant is a dinosaur to a dust mite.
        A microbe is a dinosaur to a human.
        A human is a dinosaur in waiting

391.   Some days last twenty four hours lasting twenty four days.

392.   Tonight the snow will fall and yet nothing will rise. So much for physics.

393.   Email is regular mail without the joy of discovery.
        Internet: big brother you let in willingly.
        Smart Phone: Not so smart phone

394.   Low and behold I have opened my eyes only to discover my eyes had opened

395. If you were the only girl in the world could you be a lesbian?

396. It would be easier to build another planet than convince some people that this one needs saving.

397. It is a sad fact that my popularity increases the further I retreat from my brain.

398. I am a speck on a spot on a blot on a grain in an ocean of infinity and insignificance is my name.

399. The past always clouds the future

400. Never let a good imagination be spoiled by a lousy fact.

401. I often wonder why we wander

402. I am unsure if I was taught or if I learned.

403. If three trees were felled in the forest would a conservationist make a sound?

404. I love you! I love you! Must clean that damn mirror.

405. The older I get the more I cannot tolerate all you annoying people.

406. I always tell lies!

407. The house in my head has infinite rooms but most doors remain locked.

408. I once thought that I thought original thoughts but now I think that what I once considered as original thought was in fact just repetitive thinking.

409. Open doors often let out more than they let in.

410. Whenever I am alone I realize I am not. There is comfort in knowing self.

411. On a day like today something happened several times.

412. I found the path I wish to take. Now all I need is a beginning. Time for a first step.

413. Speak not to me of what you have done; speak instead of your intentions and reasons. Then show me the results.

414. It is much easier to make stuff up than learn.

415. In the competitive world of putting on clothes things often end with a tie.

416. Have you ever wondered why and received an explanation?

417. If I take a turn to the left can I still be right?

418. Who taught Adam and Eve about sex?
　　　Did god sit them down and give them the talk or were they just up for it?

419. I once ruled the earth then woke up.

420. Send me home satisfied or take me home contented. Either will suffice.

421. The best friend to have is the one residing in your head. Contentment comes from liking one's self

422. Bullshit only comes from one place.

423. Mountains become canyons

424. Did the Titanic strike an iceberg or did an iceberg strike the Titanic.

425. No matter how hard I flap I cannot fly yet birds can walk. A lack of perspective breeds an overabundance of self-importance.

426. Life begins in light and ends in darkness as with all things in the universe.

427. My only regret is that I have a regret.

428. Never light a fuse unless you know where it leads.

429. I theorize that the argument gene has a negative effect on the hearing gene.

430. I find it amazing that it took human kind a billion years to master stupid.

431. My candle may lead the way but my match leads the candle.

432. Suppose life is sleep and sleep is life.

433. Darkness only exists because we see the light.

434.   Time ends when the clock watchers leave the room.

435.   Oranges are naturally green. Red heads are naturally orange. End of life as we know it.

436.   Consider this. The colours you see are different from those I see and yet we are able to find a middle ground. Why not with everything else?

437.   No one ever started a war because they had logically thought it through.

438.   All conflict is carried out by those unwilling to listen.

439. A pre-emptive strike is simply an idea escalated by an unreasonable assumption.

440. If you could walk on water would you tell anyone?

441. While the prosperous and poor are praying for more the ones in the middle are doing their best to either join or avoid a flock.

442. A belly flop at Bondi will eventually baste a beach in Brazil.

443. Two bees or not two bees. Maybe a wasp?

444. It's always the little stuff that becomes too heavy to carry.

445. My stomach sings with the sound of a drowning frog. Time to eat.

446. My wife doesn't understand me. That makes two of us.

447. Above us all is a concept small when you consider we reside on a ball.

448. I sit in a crowd in peace. The power of a good coffee.

449. Every time I believe I have found the meaning I am presented with a new definition.

450. Pick up line in a patisserie: a penny for your tortes.

451. Confusion comes with a non-return policy.

452. I see the light! Now where is the damn switch!

453. Would you love me more if I brought food?

454. In heaven there are many different angels. On earth there are many different angles.

455. Every bolt needs a nut!

456. Do not fear there is only me here. The rest reside inside and hide.

457. Expectation trumps realization!

458. All the attention in the world won't make a teddy bear love you. If it's stuffed it's stuffed!

459. Superiority is not standing on a tower looking down on everyone. Superiority is realizing you don't need a tower.

460. If someone in charge tells you they are acting in your best interests ask why and then go check.

461. Have a go! If you fail have another. If you still fail either change direction or have the sense to give up. Life isn't always about success.

462. Leaders rarely see the followers lining up to overtake them.

463. There are no righteous winners in war. Just luck participants.

464. The richest person on earth is still only an animal filling in time until their demise

465. Anger is the curtain that prevents the light reaching the soul.

466. Everybody urinates! A great leveller.

467. Of all the roads we may travel there is none so clearly defined as the one that leads to where we began.

468. A complete person is built one truth at a time

469. There are no individuals just loners walking paths well worn.

470. I find it amazing how easily first impressions, though usually inadequate, can be adapted to form concrete opinions.

471. An application without concept is a German manual to an Englishman.

472. A royalist believes in the status quo. A republican wants to create a new status quo to believe in. same but different.

473. The computers are staring at us!

474. Ponder for a moment that the earth instead of being the centre of everything is a lone virus in an otherwise healthy universe.

475. If the world is full of intelligent humans why then are there so many stupid questions.

476. If predictive text is so good why does it have to wait until I begin to know what I am going to say?

477. Even people who know where they are going should stop occasionally and ask for directions.

478. Prayer will give you hope. Friendship will give you comfort and support.

479. The world will always conspire to bury you. The trick is to hold out as long as possible.

480. All things can be described as either useful or useless dependent upon the users understanding of how they work.

481. Often the reason we say no is because yes will require more effort.

482. When there is nowhere left to go then be content to go nowhere.

483. The only thing that is real is our belief in reality.

484. The only thing that stands between us and extinction is nothing.

485. If you need a reason to laugh then consider this, no one else knows what it's all about either.

486. Today, as I iron, I curse the bastard who invented a wrinkling world.

487. Life, like all worthwhile endeavours is one part plan, one part dogged determination and a whole lot of luck.

488. Luck, is one part plan, one part dogged determination and a whole lot of patience.

489. The most annoying couple on the planet are a ten year old who knows everything and a sixty year old who knows he doesn't.

490. If dad says 'no' then see mum. If mum says 'no' then negotiate.

491. As children we learn valuable lessons in survival. As adults we realize those lessons could all have been categorized as luck.

492. The orange represents the earth, the pith is the crust, the zest the land we live on, the mould on the zest, the trees, the dust on the mould, us. It's that simple.

493.   If tomorrow never comes why worry about it?

494.   I never make snap judgements about people. Even idiots deserve an audience.

495.   There is great reward in silence. Especially when used in conversation.

496.   I see little point in putting my best foot forwards when it will only create resentment with the other one.

497.   People say I should show more interest in my life but the way I see it they are showing quite enough without me joining in.

498. Never assume that what you say has been heard. Ask questions, confirm. Most humans talk on loudspeaker and listen on mute.

499. Today I decided to write down only really important stuff.

500. Dear diary..... Sorry, that should have been die dearie...... always get the two mixed up.

501. Two things never to do. 1. Drive wrong way down a one way street and 2. Assume someone in politics actually has your best interests at heart.

502.   The internet is a repository of answers devoid of quantification.

503.   Ideology is the condition of the individual inflicted as a virus on the masses.

504.   It begins with a scream, survives with a struggle and will end in a whimper. Humanity.

505.   At the moment my ego is at war with my conscience. My only hope is that I end up on the side of the victor

506. House dirty and you clean it. End up with clean house. House dirty and you don't clean. End up in unliveable slum. Such is the climate change no brainer.

507. Humour, like all human conditions is curable. All you need is a dose of sensible washed down with a touch of adult.

508. Tomorrow I shall seek out the road to best. Should I fail let me at least discover the pathway to better.

509. One wonders what the world would be like if someone pushed the mute button.

510.   Is it me or does the world today seem so much more at peace with itself….. Yep, it's me.

511.   Over the hill and far away there awaits a brand new day. Never the same as the one just gone, completely different but just as long.

512.   The universe began with a bang just as the universe before that collapsed with one. Nothing comes from nothing or goes nowhere.

513.   Anger is not the stuff of logic. If we took time out to logically evaluate our reasons prior to getting angry we rarely would.

514. Have you ever wondered why people tend to leave when you start talking about yourself...... Thought not!

515. I have total faith in governments' ability to ignore the imperative in favour of the impressive.

516. Love is an investment that only pays returns based upon effort.

517. There are place in my mind where the extraordinary is normal and the impossible reality.

518. Life is all about banking memories for a time when we can no longer create new ones.

519. If the world gives you crap then save it up and use it to fertilize something new.

520. I awoke this morning and was confronted by a gravel face aggressive intruder. Note to me. Shower first, look in mirror second.

521. The basic principle of invention is taking something that already exists and modifying it to do something new.

522. Words serve but one purpose namely to plot a course to a willing listener.

523. If I look up at a billion stars I see a billion reasons to believe that we are but a magnificent accident.

524. All things have lives. Cans, rocks, rivers, rabbits. All things have lives but nothing truly ends. A beautiful quandary.

525. I use one finger to type my message on my phone. When I had a laptop I used ten. Technology has created inequality.

526. Question: do we celebrate our birthday because we arrived or because we survived.

527. Climate change may be the wrong phrase. Unchecked total planetary destruction by a self-involved dominant species would perhaps be better

528. On a lighter note, things could be worse

529. I am not stressed. I am just temporarily unable to cope with the constant pressures of my environment. Damn! I am stressed.

530. There is little joy to be had in blowing your own trumpet unless you actually play one.

531. Can it be that we are insignificant, surely not, after all we are so many.

532. Question your beliefs because answers reinforce faith. Question doubly the words of the messengers because not all convictions have merit.

533. There have been many changes during the ascent of man but the desire to tell others how to live their lives has always remained constant.

534. I once had an original idea, then a memory lapse. Nothing since.

535. The greatest motivation for all endeavours both good and bad is self. Without feelings of satisfaction or fear of defeat we would not function.

536. It's amazing how lonely one can be in a crowd.

537. Lots of things are free. The real problem is that few free things are free.

538. A healthy body is a positive; a healthy mind is an imperative. Our lives are developed, controlled and lived within our minds.

539. I used to be cynical. Now I just doubt peoples motives

540.   The bird of injustice spends most of its time feathering its own nest with the plumage of others.

541.   Why aren't there glasses that help you to focus on what is in your head.

542.   We all know there must be smarter people than ourselves out there but how do you tell who they are?

543.   Every plan is a good one until it fails.

544.   History is history unless it is used as a weapon against those caught in the

moment. Then it becomes either justice or revenge.

545. I love chocolate nearly as much as I like thinking about chocolate

546. We survived millions of years by not casually learning life skills. We survived by rote teaching. Then when it was safe to do so we went out and learnt about everything else.

547. Society can survive without you. In fact it won't miss a beat. The true joy in that is the realization that you can survive without society.

548. Our minds are content downloaded computers. Choose your programmers carefully.

549. Has there been just one moment when you thought 'what's it all about'? Has the question haunted you? That is the true seed of human progress.

550. One of the greatest threats to an ordered society is people's ability to grasp a basic concept and then fill in the details with assumption.

551. No one can blow out your candle. Some may well try but in the end it all comes to your willingness to protect your own light.

552. Friend of mine tripped the other day. I laughed. My bruised shoulder indicates that laughter may not be the best medicine.

553. I buy lottery tickets in the expectation of a win. I check the results with expectation of a loss. What does that indicate?

554. Looking at our speed of true innovation and not simply reinvention I propose that we have a better chance of deleting ourselves from existence than populating other worlds.

555. Evil people can only survive in the darkness of complacency.

556. On day I shall run out of words and have nothing to ………

557. Does gravity push us down or pull us down?

558. It takes just one genuine asylum seeker handed back to their government to make a morally bankrupt society.

559. Are my cats, as they sleep out their day, living fulfilling lives? If so where is their reality? In their six hour awake world or in their eighteen hour sleeping minds?

560. If you want to feel young again forget Botox or beauty treatments and just go sit with older people.

561. Is growing old gracefully similar to getting run over willingly?

562. There are two types of minds. Manuals and automatics. Manuals are always seeking the correct gear, automatics never find it.

563. There are many roads to heaven. Unfortunately they all begin with your demise.

564. When I was young the expectation was that I act grown up. Sadly, now that I am much older I still get chided for being childish

565. The line down the middle of the road denotes which side to stay on as does the line denoting appropriateness. Alas, it's a two way street.

566. There is little point in the deliverer being blunt if the recipient isn't sharp.

567. For every way of doing something right there are at least ten ways of doing it wrong. Patience breeds success.

568. It is said that two can play at that game. What isn't said is that only one can win.

569. I am going to be famous as soon as I master competent.

570. We made time! We carved up the daylight into clockwork rules, combined that into weekly regulations then dragged the whole lot into yearly laws and we have been its slave ever since.

571. Never be fooled by the publicity. Society is always about those with all the stuff employing those with no stuff to make more stuff for stuff all pay.

572. Confidence is the ability to irrationally suspend fear of failure in favour of an unreasonable expectation of success

573. The last thing you expect is the last thing you expect.

574. I am much larger in mind than in person.

575. There are no beginnings or endings just endless journeys

576. Thought is like flowing water moving freely until it encounters an obstacle where it circles until it finds a way forwards. Fluid and unstoppable.

577. The first words we say are usually the ones that get us into the trouble that we have to spend tomes getting out of.

578. A joke is a picture of absurdity drawn in the mind of the listener.

579. If you tell the truth and ten people don't believe you is it still the truth?

580. The internet is humankind's supreme achievement when it comes to conservation because all of the rubbish keeps getting recycled forever.

581. A person's existence cannot be defined without also defining those who were there before, during and after.

582. I want more! No damn it I want it all! And then when I finally have everything I want to use it to help those with nothing!

583. Never let a bad plan ruin a good idea.

584. As a species we tell ourselves that we are superior to all other things around us. Problem is we are the only ones saying that.

585. I find it amazing that political leaders always have the answers but rarely the solutions.

586. Why are children's voices always turned up and their hearing always turned down.

587. Where in the bible does it say, "thou shall not ask questions about what is in the bible"

588. Sit on hills, watch sunrises, listen to the world, be you.

589. Could it be that the only universe I am the centre of is mine. Surely not. After all, from where I stand I am at the middle of everything.

590. Is it righteous people or 'right are us' people?

591. Everybody needs one friend and one arsehole. What you don't need is for them to be the same person.

592. A rule is a guideline used to achieve balance. A regulation is a law used to achieve compliance. People use rules, governments use regulations.

593. Oh look, my left foot just fell off! Anything for attention.
    It's alright I managed to put it on again but it still really hurts! Anything for sympathy.

594. I ponder the chances of seeing a blimp shaped like a cow drift by. I conclude, once in a moo balloon.

595. My quest, should I be permitted to have one, is to find out why so many people insist on going on damn quests.

596. The greatest threat to democracy lies in the individual politician's inability to put personal conviction before party.

597. The world is round or flat. The difference only lies in the perspective of the eagle or ant.

598. Do you choose to scratch your nose then do it or scratch your nose and realize you are doing it?

599. The sun is leaving, the rain is coming, the fire is burning, I am bunkering, perfect.

600. Much can be said about very little.

601. Money, power, politics and self-interest are the four witches of climate change. Pain, suffering, death and extinction are their most powerful spells.

602. There are more synapsis in your brain than visible stars in the night sky. What does that tell you about size

603. The real satisfaction in writing lies in the effort taken to put pen to paper. Should you get published, sell a million copies, get rich, famous and die a national treasure that's just icing on the cake!

Yeah! Right!

The End

www.ingramcontent.com/pod-product-compliance
Lightning Source LLC
Chambersburg PA
CBHW031424210526
45464CB00005B/2045